POWERFUL ARMORED VEHICLES

Lynn Peppas

Crabtree Publishing Company

www.crabtreebooks.com

Created by Bobbie Kalman

Author
Lynn Peppas

Editor
Adrianna Morganelli

Proofreader
Kathy Middleton

Photo research
Samara Parent
Crystal Sikkens

Design
Samara Parent

**Production coordinator
and prepress technician**
Samara Parent

Print coordinator
Katherine Berti

Photographs
Alamy: © ITAR-TASS Photo Agency: pages 26, 27
BAE Systems: page 30
Keystone Press: wenn.com: page 18
Thierry Lachapelle/worldwide-defence.blogspot.com: page 19
Lockheed Martin: page 31
Shutterstock: pages 1, 3, 8–9
United States Army: page 13; Pennsylvania National Guard: page 28; Marie
        Berberea, U.S. Fires Center of Excellence: page 29
U.S. Marine Corps photo by CPL R.P. Tudor: front cover
Wikimedia Commons: Bundeswehr_Fotos: pages 4–5; Fiorellino: page 6;
        MathKnight and Zachi Evenor: pages 7, 20–21; Specialist Thornberny (U.S.
        Army): page 10; Marine Force's Europe Operation/Exercise/Event: GTEP: page
        11; U.S. Army: pages 13, 14, 16; U.S. Military: page 15; TSGT Mike Buytas,
        USAF: page 17 (top and bottom); U.S. Navy photo by Mass Communication
        Specialist 2nd Class Sandra M. Palumbo: page 17 (center); Alvaro Aro, U. S.
        Marine Corps: pages 22–23; U.S. Air Force photo/James M. Bowman: page 24;
        Joe Bullinger, U.S. Navy: page 25

Front cover: A LAV-25 light armored vehicle from Company A, 3rd Light
Armored Vehicle Battalion, is picked up by a CH-53E Super Stallion helicopter
for transport.
Back cover: Three Leopard 2 A5 tanks from the German Army
Title page: A camouflage army Stryker

Library and Archives Canada Cataloguing in Publication

Peppas, Lynn
    Powerful armored vehicles / Lynn Peppas.

(Vehicles on the move)
Includes index.
Issued also in electronic formats.
ISBN 978-0-7787-2750-7 (bound).--ISBN 978-0-7787-2755-2 (pbk.)

    1. Armored vehicles, Military--Juvenile literature.
I. Title. II. Series: Vehicles on the move

UG446.5.P46 2011   j623.74'75   C2011-906689-0

Library of Congress Cataloging-in-Publication Data

Peppas, Lynn.
    Powerful armored vehicles / Lynn Peppas.
        p. cm. -- (Vehicles on the move)
    Includes index.
    ISBN 978-0-7787-2750-7 (reinforced library binding : alk. paper) -- ISBN
    978-0-7787-2755-2 (pbk. : alk. paper) -- ISBN 978-1-4271-9925-6 (electronic
    pdf) -- ISBN 978-1-4271-9930-0 (electronic html)
    1. Armored vehicles, Military--Juvenile literature. I. Title. II. Series.

    UG446.5.P36 2012
    623.74'75--dc23
                                            2011039601

Crabtree Publishing Company

www.crabtreebooks.com   1-800-387-7650

Printed in the U.S.A./112011/JA20111018

**Published in Canada
Crabtree Publishing**
616 Welland Ave.
St. Catharines, Ontario
L2M 5V6

**Published in the United States
Crabtree Publishing**
PMB 59051
350 Fifth Avenue, 59th Floor
New York, New York 10118

**Published in the United Kingdom
Crabtree Publishing**
Maritime House
Basin Road North, Hove
BN41 1WR

**Published in Australia
Crabtree Publishing**
3 Charles Street
Coburg North
VIC 3058

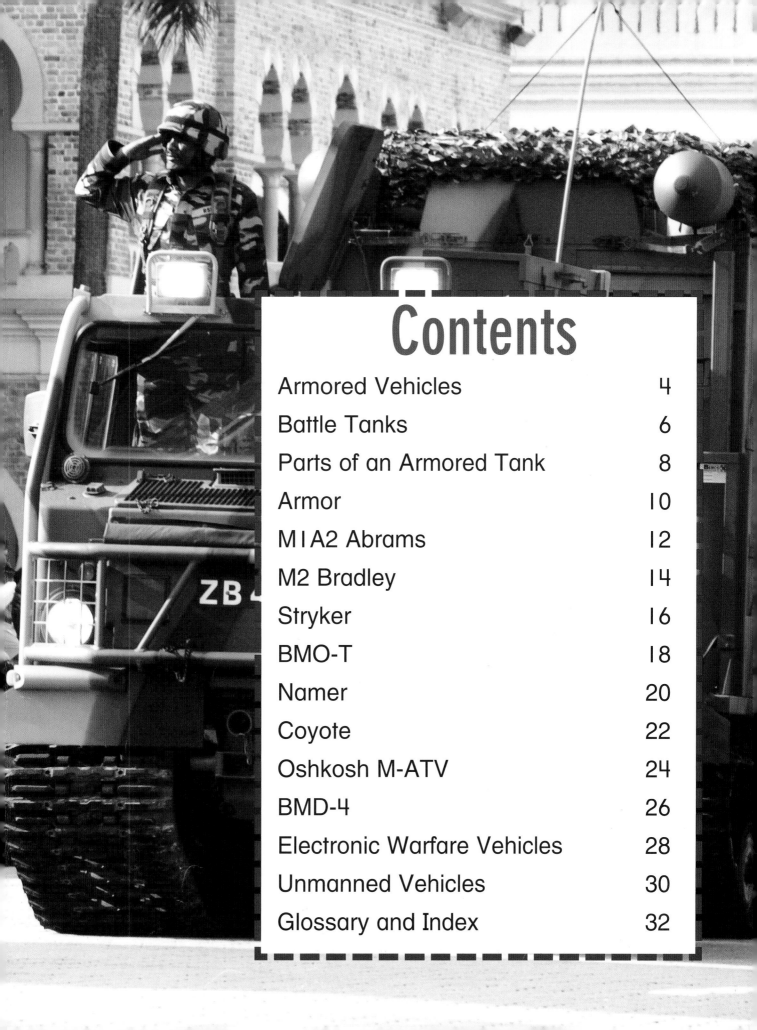

Contents

Armored Vehicles

Armored military vehicles are used to fight **enemy** forces. Vehicles are machines that can move and do work. Armored vehicles are used during **combat**. Armor is the outer cover that protects vehicles and the soldiers inside them from **ammunition** fired at them.

The Leopard 2 tank is being used in battle by Canadian armed forces in Afghanistan.

Armed forces need different kinds of armored vehicles for ground **warfare**. Some armored vehicles carry weapons such as machine guns and cannons. Armored trucks move supplies and troops to where they need to go. Many are camouflaged, which means they are painted the same color as their surroundings. Camouflage makes them hard to see.

Battle Tanks

Battle tanks are the most heavily armored military vehicles. Battle tanks fight on the front lines where the fighting is. They attack enemy forces on the ground. Some battle tanks are used to gather information about the enemy. A tank's armor, weapons, and ammunition make them very heavy. Many weigh over 50 tons (45 metric tons).

The Challenger 2 tank was used in battle by the United Kingdom's armed forces in Iraq.

A tank comes ready for battle. It has a large main gun and other weapons, such as machine guns. Most tanks need a crew of four people. There is not a lot of room inside for the crew. Sometimes a crew lives inside the tank for many days at a time.

Tanks have powerful engines that help them travel at speeds up to 50 mph (80 km/h).

Parts of an Armored Tank

The driver sits inside the hull, or lower body, of the tank underneath the main gun. He or she sees outside by looking through a periscope. Periscopes show what is going on around the tank on the outside. Night vision equipment is used by drivers to see at night without using lights. This way the enemy won't spot them. The equipment "sees" things by the heat they give off. The turret is a structure for weapons on top of the hull. It can move in a complete circle. The main gun and machine guns are on the turret and can be aimed in any direction.

main gun

track

Tanks move on two tracks made up of many metal links called treads. Treads are able to move on rough and slippery surfaces such as sand, mud, and rocks. The wide tracks spread the tank's weight more evenly on the ground so it is less likely to sink on soft land.

machine gun

periscope

turret hatch

driver's hatch

turret

hull

Armor

Armor can protect a vehicle and the people inside from enemy bullets, shells, missiles, and grenades. Armored vehicles are made from thick steel. Sometimes steel is mixed with other materials such as ceramic, metal, or plastic to give it extra strength. Some tanks have special liners inside that stop small flying pieces of the tank from harming the crew if there is an explosion.

The M1 Abrams tanks now have stronger armor on all sides of the tank. This helps keep soliders inside the tank safer.

Armored vehicles are tough to destroy. New ammunitions are always being invented to pierce, or break through, armor. Some tanks have a special armor called Explosive Reactive Armor (ERA). Plates of ERA sit on top of the armored tank. The ERA plates create their own explosion to damage incoming ammunition when it hits the tank.

Sloped sides, or sides on an angle, also help protect the vehicle when it gets hit. Sloped sides are harder for ammunition to break through.

MIA2 Abrams

The MIA2 Abrams is the main battle tank of the U.S. Army. It is protected with a very hard armor made of steel and ceramic. The front of the hull and turret have extra armor. Some MIA2 Abrams have equipment that detects, or discovers, **guided missiles** coming toward them. The system jams, or mixes up, the missile's **signal** and throws it off course so the missile does not hit the tank.

Family members of soldiers get to explore the MIA2 Abrams tanks in Fort Hood, Texas.

The M1A2 Abrams has a main gun and three machine guns. Four crew members are needed to operate it. It runs on different kinds of fuel such as gas, diesel, kerosene, and even jet fuel.

The M1A2 Abrams weighs over 62 tons (56 metric tons) and can travel at speeds up to 42 mph (67 km/h).

M2 Bradley

The M2 Bradley is a fighting vehicle. Its job is to bring soldiers to a battleground and fight enemy forces. Besides a crew of three people, it can also carry six soldiers and their weapons.

The M2 Bradley is an amphibious vehicle. Amphibious means it can move on ground or in water. On water it can go about 4 mph (7 km/h). It is much faster on land and can travel at speeds up to 41 mph (66 km/h).

The M2 Bradley can use its tracks to move through water.

Stryker

Not all armored vehicles run on tracks. The Stryker is an armored fighting vehicle with eight wheels. It needs a crew of only one driver and one **commander**. The commander also does the job of gunner if needed.

A Stryker can carry nine soldiers and their weapons.

The Stryker is used to carry soldiers and fight enemy forces. The Stryker is protected with ceramic armor. The bottom of the vehicle has extra armor to protect it from mine blasts. A machine gun, **grenade launcher**, and other equipment are mounted onto the top. As far as tanks go, it is very fast and can travel at speeds up to 62 mph (100 km/h).

(top) The weapons and equipment on the Stryker are controlled by a soldier (center).

Slat armor is a steel cage that is fastened to the outside of the Stryker. This protects it from grenades.

BMO-T

The BMO-T is a heavy armor tank used to carry troops and their weapons into battle. They move special teams of ground soldiers that carry rocket launchers on their backs. The rocket launcher is called a bumblebee. It shoots rockets at enemy sites or vehicles.

Soldiers sometimes use a bumblebee rocket launcher, which is also known as a "Shmel."

The BMO-T is built in Russia. It has Explosive Reactive Armor panels built into it. The BMO-T runs on tracks and can carry 32 rocket launchers inside. It takes a crew of two people to run it and can also carry seven other soldiers. The tank can move at speeds up to 37 mph (60 km/h).

Namer

The Namer is one of the best protected personnel carrier tanks in the world. It has armor made of steel mixed with ceramic. The Namer also has a system that protects the crew from nuclear, biological, and chemical weapons, or NBC. Called **weapons of mass destruction**, NBC weapons could harm people for many miles around the target. The Namer has an air filter that screens out the harmful **toxins** from NBC weapons.

It takes a crew of two people to operate the Namer. It can also carry ten other soldiers. It has two machine guns and a grenade launcher. The Namer travels at speeds up to 37 mph (60 km/h).

The Namer is built and used in Israel. Namer means "leopard" in Hebrew. Hebrew is the main language spoken in Israel.

אין לטפס
על הכלי

Coyote

The Coyote is an armored vehicle that is used to watch and gather information about an area. They must be light and quick to get the job done. They run on eight wheels and can travel at speeds up to 62 mph (100 km/h). They weigh over 14 tons (12 metric tons).

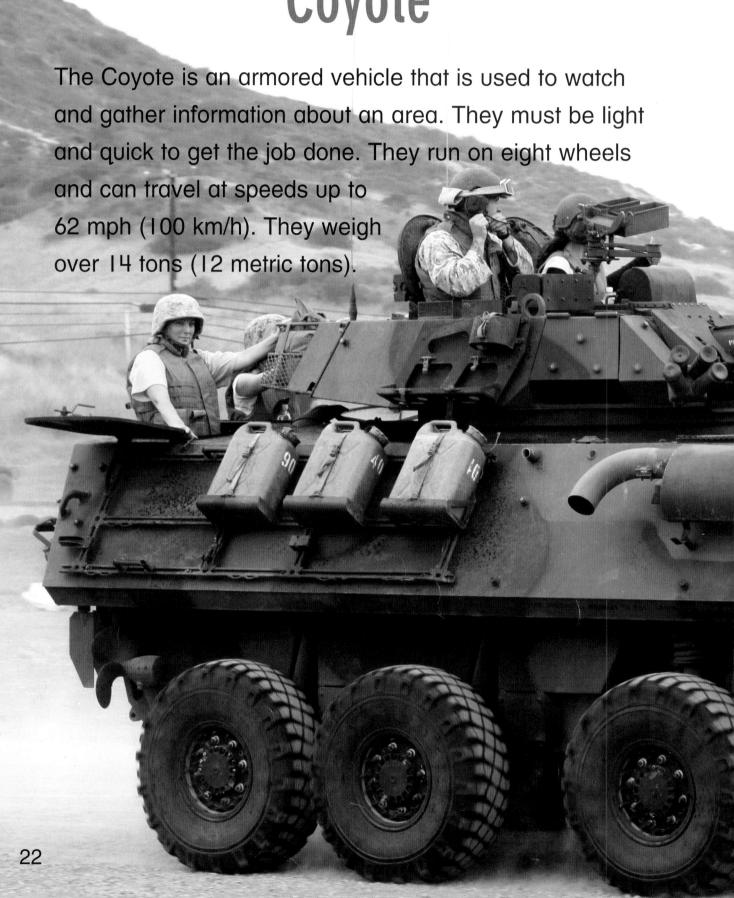

The Coyote has slanting side and front panels that protect it from enemy fire. Slanted panels are harder to pierce with ammunition, which can even bounce off. Armor panels can be added to the Coyote to protect it from larger ammunition such as grenades. The vehicle is armed with a main gun and two smaller machine guns. It has electronic **surveillance** equipment that can find out information about enemy forces.

*The Coyote's radar can **detect** large vehicles such as trucks almost 15 miles (24 km) away from it.*

Oshkosh M-ATV

ATV stands for all-terrain vehicle. All-terrain means it can travel over most ground conditions. The Oshkosh M-ATV is an MRAP vehicle. MRAP stands for Mine Resistant Ambush Protected. An ambush is a surprise attack from a hidden area. The M-ATV is protected from explosions by land mines or roadside bombs.

Oshkosh M-ATVs are light enough to be moved from one area to another by aircraft.

The Oshkosh M-ATV weighs over 14 tons (12 metric tons) but is very lightweight for an armored vehicle. It can travel at speeds up to 75 mph (120 km/h). The M-ATV has four tires that are able to keep from going flat for many miles after being pierced. This vehicle costs just under half a million dollars.

An Oshkosh M-ATV can be armed with a machine gun or grenade launcher.

BMD-4

The BMD-4 is an armored vehicle that is easy to transport from one area to another. It is made in Russia for the Russian military. The BMD-4 does not have as much armor as other armored fighting vehicles. This keeps the vehicle light enough to be transported by aircraft. It weighs only 13.5 tons (12.2 metric tons).

The BMD-4 can be dropped from an aircraft using a parachute.

The BMD-4 is armed with a cannon, machine guns, and missile and grenade launchers. It is an amphibious vehicle. In the water it is very slow and travels at six mph (10 km/h). On land it can travel at speeds up to 44 mph (70 km/h).

It takes three crew members to operate the BMD-4. It can also hold up to five fully equipped soldiers.

Electronic Warfare Vehicles

Electronic warfare vehicles use **electronics** to do important jobs for troops who are fighting on the ground. Some vehicles carry electronic systems that help keep soldiers safe, such as the CREW Duke system. The CREW Duke system is mounted to a vehicle. It can block a signal being sent to make a roadside bomb or land mine explode.

The equipment used to block signals must be checked often to make sure it is working properly.

The MEWSS is an electronic warfare vehicle that spies on the enemy. The MEWSS has special equipment that can find out information such as the enemy's location. It can also send signals that mix up the enemy's information-gathering systems. The MEWSS can travel on both water and land. It travels at six mph (10 km/h) on water and up to 62 mph (100 km/h) on land. The vehicle weighs over 12 tons (10 metric tons) and can be carried by aircraft.

Soldiers must take courses to learn how to operate the electronic warfare systems.

Unmanned Vehicles

The Black Knight is an unmanned military tank. Unmanned means that it operates without people inside it. The Black Knight is like a robot and is controlled by a commander inside another tank such as the M2 Bradley. It does very dangerous jobs such as scouting, gathering information on the enemy, or going into risky combat areas.

The Black Knight has a main gun and a machine gun. It can travel up to 48 mph (77 km/h).

The SMSS is the largest unmanned vehicle ever used in battle by U.S. soldiers. It is used to carry equipment, such as supplies and weapons. It can carry up to 1200 pounds (544 kg). The SMSS is a like a robot that follows the soldiers around. It can identify the soldiers by their **3-D** shape.

SMSS vehicles are built to follow soldiers wherever they go, even through water.

Glossary

3-D Involving three dimensions

ammunition Bullets, shells, rockets, or other explosive devices that are fired from a gun or launcher

armed forces A country's group of soldiers who fight on the ground, at sea, and in the air

combat To fight against an enemy

commander The person in charge of a military force or unit

detect To find out or discover

electronics Referring to electronic devices or systems

enemy A force that works against a person or a country

grenade launcher A device that shoots grenades that are filled with explosive, poisoned gases

guided missile An explosive ammunition that is fired but follows a course toward a particular target

weapons of mass destruction Weapons that destroy all living things over a large area

signal A sign that tells or communicates a message

toxin Something that is poisonous

surveillance Close watch over a person or area

warfare An armed conflict or fighting against an army

Index